AMAZING NATIONAL PARKS

GRAND CANYON

National Park

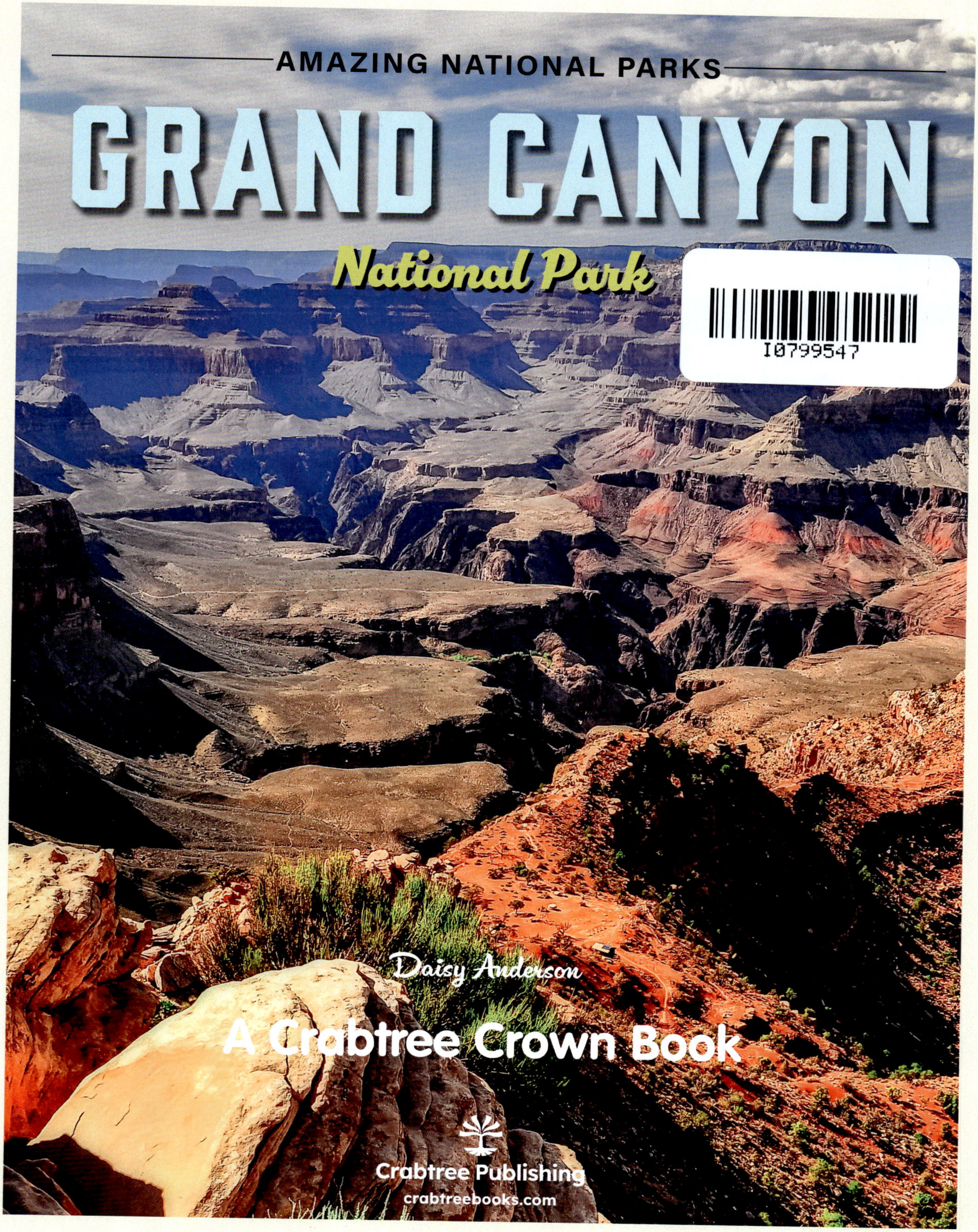

Daisy Anderson

A Crabtree Crown Book

Crabtree Publishing
crabtreebooks.com

School-to-Home Support for Caregivers and Teachers

This appealing book is designed to teach students about core subject areas. Students will build upon what they already know about the subject, and engage in topics that they want to learn more about. Here are a few guiding questions to help readers build their comprehension skills. Possible answers appear here in red.

Before Reading:

What do I know about Grand Canyon National Park?

- *I know the national park is a huge canyon.*
- *I know many people visit Grand Canyon National Park.*

What do I want to learn about this topic?

- *I want to learn what people can see in the national park.*
- *I want to learn what people can do in the national park.*

During Reading:

I'm curious to know...

- *I'm curious to know what kinds of desert animals live in the national park.*
- *I'm curious to know if people can go to the bottom of the canyon.*

How is this like something I already know?

- *I know some snakes live in the desert.*
- *I know the canyon is deep.*

After Reading:

What was the author trying to teach me?

- *The author was trying to teach me about why so many people visit Grand Canyon National Park.*
- *The author was trying to teach me what visitors can see at the national park.*

How did the photographs and captions help me understand more?

- *The photographs helped me picture what the national park looks like.*
- *The captions gave me extra information about the history of Grand Canyon National Park.*

TABLE OF CONTENTS

Chapter 1

WELCOME TO GRAND CANYON NATIONAL PARK

Layers of brightly colored rock show the power of water and time. The Grand **Canyon** is one of the seven natural wonders of the world. It's also a national park that millions of people visit every year!

Know the Park

The U.S. government owns national parks and takes care of them. National parks are used to help protect natural areas.

Know the Park

The North Rim and the South Rim are two sides at the top of the canyon. Driving from the South Rim to the North Rim takes about five hours.

Grand Canyon National Park includes more than 1,900 square miles (4,921 square kilometers) of land. The Grand Canyon itself is 277 miles (446 kilometers) long. Grand Canyon National Park is in Arizona. The Colorado River runs through the canyon.

BEFORE IT WAS A PARK

Native Americans first lived on canyon lands thousands of years ago. The Navajo, Southern Paiute, Hualapai, Hopi, Zuni, Apache, and Havasupai all think of the Grand Canyon as a **sacred** place. Only the Havasupai people still live in a village in the Grand Canyon.

The Havasupai have lived in Supai Village in the Grand Canyon for more than 1,000 years—and still do!

Explorers from Europe first visited the Grand Canyon in the 1500s but did not settle there. Some copper mining was done in the area in the late 1800s. Word spread that the Grand Canyon was a special natural area. It became a popular place to visit in the early 1900s.

FOUNDING THE PARK

Many people in the United States government worked to protect the Grand Canyon. President Benjamin Harrison first named it a protected area in 1893. President Theodore Roosevelt made the Grand Canyon a **national monument** in 1908. The U.S. Congress passed a bill to make it a national park on February 26, 1919.

President Roosevelt rode a mule to the bottom of the Grand Canyon in 1903.

THE PARK TODAY

Grand Canyon National Park is the 11th-largest national park in the United States. It has 595 miles (957 kilometers) of trails. Between 4 to 6 million people enjoy Grand Canyon National Park every year!

Chapter 2

THE LAND AND CLIMATE

The Grand Canyon is part of an area called the Colorado **plateau**. It was formed between 70 and 30 million years ago when **tectonic plates** pushed together and **uplifted** the rock. The Colorado River ran through the plateau. The river began carving the Grand Canyon 5 to 6 million years ago.

Know the Park

The Grand Canyon's rock is in layers from youngest to oldest. The youngest rock at the top formed about 270 million years ago. The rock at the bottom is 1.8 billion years old.

Over millions of years, the Colorado River's waters chipped away at the rock and cut into the earth to create the canyon. Rain, snow, and ice **eroded** the canyon's sides and made them wider. Water continues to widen and carve out the canyon today.

There are no dinosaur fossils in the Grand Canyon—the rock formed long before they existed!

CLIMATE

Temperatures at the Grand Canyon depend on the **elevation**. The lowest areas have the highest temperatures. It may be 70 °F (21 °C) on the rim but 100 °F (38 °C) at the floor of the canyon at the same time. The Grand Canyon is so wide and so deep that it has more than one **climate**. The top of the Grand Canyon is a mountain region. The bottom, called the inner canyon, is a desert.

Know the Park

The Grand Canyon is 18 miles (29 kilometers) across at its widest part. The canyon floor is 4,800 feet (1,463 meters) below the South Rim and about 6,000 feet (1,828 meters) below the North Rim.

Know the Park

Thunderstorms may happen during any season in the national park. Lightning strikes there about 25,000 times per year. Heavy rain may cause flash floods in the canyon.

The rims have rain in the summer and snow in the winter. It snows up to 58 inches (147 cm) on the South Rim every year. The North Rim is colder and sees about 142 inches (360 cm) of snow. But it snows less than 1 inch (2.5 cm) in the inner canyon.

Chapter 3

PLANTS IN THE PARK

Woodlands cover the Grand Canyon's rim. Ponderosa pine forests are found at the highest elevation. Pinyon pine and Utah juniper trees grow lower down. Some areas also have spruce and fir trees.

Know the Park

Ponderosa pines may live to be more than 400 years old. The North Rim has some of the oldest trees in Arizona.

Yucca plants have thick skin and roots to hold water.

The inner canyon is a desert region. Twenty-five **species** of cactuses are found in the national park. Most grow in the inner canyon. Desert plants such as banana yucca and big sagebrush also grow there. But not all of the inner canyon is dry. Cottonwood and willow trees thrive on the banks of the Colorado River.

FLOWERING PLANTS

About 650 kinds of wildflowers color the national park. Lupines show off their purple blossoms. Globemallows have orange flowers shaped like cups. These wildflowers and many more bloom on the rim from March to May.

Grand Canyon cactuses bloom in many colors. They flower from March to June. The prickly pear cactus may have yellow, pink, orange, or red blossoms. The flowers become a berry-like fruit eaten by many animals.

Groups of prickly pear cactuses provide shelter for birds and rattlesnakes.

Chapter 4

ANIMALS IN THE PARK

Forest animals such as elk, squirrels, and mule deer live in the woodlands along the rim. Mountain lions hunt in the forests of both the North and South Rim. Almost 450 kinds of birds have been spotted at Grand Canyon National Park.

Know the Park

The area around the Grand Canyon is one place where the rare California condor is found. This bird was brought back into the wild in the 1990s after nearly becoming **extinct**. Today more than 70 live in the area.

Know the Park

Rattlesnakes live in the inner canyon, but some are also found on the rim. Visitors should never go near a rattlesnake.

ANIMALS OF THE INNER CANYON

Desert animals live in the inner canyon. Reptiles such as chuckwallas and yellow-backed spiny lizards enjoy the heat. The area is also home to six kinds of rattlesnakes. The Grand Canyon rattlesnake is found nowhere else in the world.

Bald eagles are seen near open water or rivers.

ALONG THE RIVER

The Colorado River supports many kinds of wildlife. Coyotes and bobcats hunt rabbits and other small animals along its banks. Many species of birds nest along the river. Others **migrate** through the area as the seasons change. Bald eagles hunt for trout in the river during winter.

WATCHING WILDLIFE

Many animals of the Grand Canyon are most active at dawn or at dusk. It's important to remember that all are wild. Keeping your distance and watching through binoculars or by zooming in with your camera is the safest way to enjoy the wildlife.

People should stay at least 6 feet (1.8 meters) from the edge of the Grand Canyon when taking photos.

Chapter 5
TIPS ON WHAT TO SEE

Know the Park

The visitor center and lodges are part of Grand Canyon Village on the South Rim. The village also has buildings that date from the early 1900s.

THE SOUTH RIM

The South Rim is the most popular side. Visitors can look out over the Grand Canyon from Mather Point, which is wheelchair friendly. Park rangers at the visitor center help people plan hikes. Visitors may also book rooms in lodges that have views of the canyon.

DESERT VIEW DRIVE

Desert View Drive is the only **scenic** road for cars along the South Rim. It begins near Grand Canyon Village and goes for 23 miles (37 kilometers). The drive has six places where cars can stop and look out over the Grand Canyon and the Colorado River. It also has four picnic areas.

Know the Park

Desert View Watchtower is a 70-foot (21-meter) tall stone building that looks east over the Grand Canyon. Visitors may climb to its upper floors.

HERMIT ROAD

Visitors can ride a free shuttle bus from Grand Canyon Village along Hermit Road for more views of the canyon. The road is 7 miles (11 kilometers) long and the bus stops at nine places. Canyon Rim Trail follows alongside Hermit Road and can be hiked.

THE NORTH RIM

Only 10 percent of park visitors go to the North Rim, so it's less crowded. It has one lodge and one campground. Visitors can hike a short trail to Bright Angel Point for views from the other side of the canyon.

The trail to Bright Angel Point is short but steep.

Chapter 6

TIPS ON WHAT TO DO

Know the Park

Visitors to the national park should follow the Leave No Trace Principles. They include staying on trails, leaving no trash behind, and treating wildlife with respect.

HIKING

Hiking can be one of the best ways to see the Grand Canyon. Some trails are short and go to scenic viewpoints along the rim. But there are no easy trails into or out of the canyon itself. Hikers should plan carefully and carry lots of water.

Know the Park

Phantom Ranch is at the bottom of the Grand Canyon. It has a lodge and cabins. It can be reached by hiking, by mule, or by rafting the Colorado River.

MULE RIDES

Guided mule rides are a popular way to see the Grand Canyon without walking. Some trail rides go along the rim and last for two hours. Others are overnight trips and travel deep into the canyon.

RAFTING

Many enjoy rafting trips through the Grand Canyon on the Colorado River. These guided trips may last a half day, a full day, or even as long as 18 days.

Experienced guides are needed to raft the Grand Canyon. The river has 250 rapids!

Whether you visit the South Rim, the North Rim, or both, Grand Canyon National Park is a special place to see!

GLOSSARY

canyon (KAN-yuhn): A deep valley with steep sides and often a stream or river running through it

climate (KLYE-mit): The usual weather conditions of a place over a long period of time

elevation (el-uh-VAY-shun): The height of a place above sea level

eroded (ih-ROAD-ed): Worn away over time by water and wind

extinct (ek-STINGKT): No longer existing

migrate (MYE-grate): To move from one area to another at a particular time of year

national monument (NASH-uh-nl MON-uh-ment): Land or historic area that has been given permanent protection by the U.S. president or Congress

plateau (pla-TOH): An area of flat land that is higher than the land around it

sacred (SAY-krid): Holy, or very important and deserving of great respect

scenic (SEE-nik): Having beautiful natural surroundings

species (SPEE-seez): A group of animals or plants that are similar and can reproduce with one another

tectonic plates (tek-TAA-nuhk playts): The flat, rocky pieces that make up Earth's outer crust

uplift (UHP-lift): An increase in the vertical elevation of Earth's surface as a result of natural causes

INDEX

COMPREHENSION QUESTIONS

1. Grand Canyon National Park is in ____.
   a. Utah
   b. California
   c. Arizona
2. The inner canyon is a ____ region.
   a. desert
   b. woodland
   c. mountain
3. The ____ River runs through the national park.
   a. Mississippi
   b. Rio Grande
   c. Colorado
4. True or False: The North Rim is the side most people visit.
5. True or False: The Grand Canyon is so wide and so deep that it has more than one climate.

Answers: 1. C, 2. A, 3. C, 4.False, 5. True

ABOUT THE AUTHOR

Daisy Anderson loves to write real-life books for curious kids. She lives in the Midwest, where she enjoys exploring the great outdoors with her two dogs. When Daisy isn't writing, she's out hiking and having fun in nature.

Written by: Daisy Anderson
Designed by: Bobbie Houser
Series Development: James Earley
Proofreader: Melissa Boyce
Educational Consultant: Marie Lemke M.Ed.

Photographs:
t = Top, c = Center, b = Bottom, l = Left, r = Right

Alamy: US Marines Photo: p. 6; Natural History Archive: p. 7, 8

Shutterstock: Martin M303: cover, p. 1; CK Foto: p. 4; Beth Ruggiero-York: p. 5 t; Globe Turner: p. 5 b; Tupungato: p. 9; Georgi Baird: p. 10-11; Traci L. Hardin: p. 12; LHBLLC: p. 13; Sergey Malomuzh: p. 14; Nikki Yancey: p. 15; Motmot: p. 16 l; Chris Hill: p. 16 r; David G Hayes: p. 17; Shaylin Tombs: p. 18; Gordon Montgomery: p. 19; Steve Jamsa: p. 20; Maridav: p. 21; INTREEGUE Photography: p. 22; OLOS: p. 23; meunierd: p. 24; Mike Buchheit: p. 25; Galyna Andrushko: p. 26; Studio Barcelona: p. 27; Jim Mallouk: p. 28-29

Crabtree Publishing

crabtreebooks.com 800-387-7650

Printed in Canada/012025/CP20250101

Published in Canada
Crabtree Publishing
616 Welland Ave.
St. Catharines, Ontario
L2M 5V6

Published in the United States
Crabtree Publishing
347 Fifth Ave
Suite 1402-145
New York, NY 10016

Library and Archives Canada Cataloguing in Publication
Available at Library and Archives Canada

Library of Congress Cataloging-in-Publication Data
Available at the Library of Congress

Hardcover: 978-1-0398-6483-2
Paperback: 978-1-0398-6552-5
Ebook (pdf): 978-1-0398-6621-8
Epub: 978-1-0398-6690-4